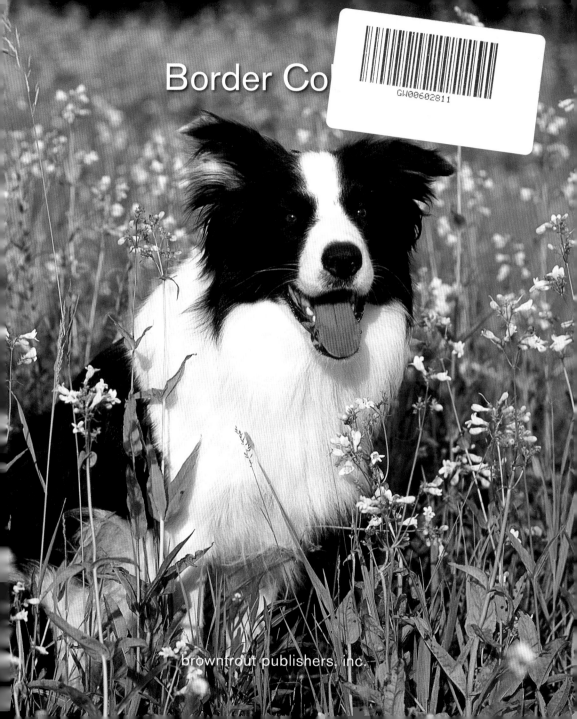

Border Co[llie]

GW00602811

browntrout publishers, inc.

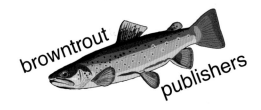

www.browntrout.com

INTERNATIONAL AFFILIATES

UNITED KINGDOM

BrownTrout Publishers Ltd.
P.O. Box 201
Bristol BS99 5ZE England UK
(44) 117 317 1880
UK Freephone: 0800 169 3718
sales@browntroutuk.com

AUSTRALIA

BrownTrout Publishers Pty. Ltd.
12 Mareno Road
Tullamarine VIC 3043, Australia
03 9338 4766
Outside Australia: (61) 3 9338 4766
Australia Toll Free: 1 800 111 882
sales@browntrout.com.au

CANADA

BrownTrout Publishers Ltd.
5 Douglas Street, Unit 201
The Gummer Building
Guelph ON N1H 2S8, Canada
(1) 519 821 8882
Canada Toll Free: 1 888 254 5842
Fax: (1) 519 821 1012
sales@browntrout.ca

JAPAN

BrownTrout Publishers Japan, Ltd.
209-4 5 Chome,
Ishikawa-cho, Naka-ku
Yokohama-shi, Japan
(81) 90 1858 3142
Fax: (82) 31 281 3362
sales@browntrout.co.jp

MEXICO

Editorial SalmoTruti, SA de CV
Hegel 153 Int. 903, Colonia Polanco,
Del. Miguel Hidalgo, 11560 Mexico D.F.,
Mexico
(52-55) 5545 0492
Mexico Toll Free: 01 800 716 7420
ventas@salmotruti.com.mx

NEW ZEALAND

BrownTrout Publishers Ltd.
P.O. Box 65 542
Mairangi Bay, Auckland, New Zealand
(64) 09 478 1520
New Zealand Toll Free: 0800 888 112
sales@browntrout.net.nz

KOREA

BrownTrout Publishers Korea Ltd.
A-Dong, Room# 103, Hyang Rin Villa
84-19 Dongbaek-Ri, Gusung-Eup
Yongin-si, Gyeonggi-do
449-911 Korea
(82) 31 281 3363
Fax: (82) 31 281 3362
sales@browntrout.co.kr

2008 YEAR PLANNER

JANUARY			FEBRUARY			MARCH			APRIL		
1 TUE	C/L	BRD	1 FRI			1 SAT	OFF		1 TUE		
2 WED	C/L	B/E	2 SAT	OFF		2 SUN	OFF		2 WED		
3 THU	C/L	B/E	3 SUN	OFF		3 MON			3 THU		
4 FRI	C/L	B/E	4 MON			4 TUE			4 FRI		
5 SAT	OFF	OFF	5 TUE			5 WED			5 SAT	WORKING	
6 SUN	OFF	OFF	6 WED			6 THU			6 SUN	WORKING	
7 MON	C/E	OFF	7 THU			7 FRI			7 MON		
8 TUE	C/E	B/E	8 FRI			8 SAT	WORKING		8 TUE		
9 WED	C/RD	B/E	9 SAT	WORKING		9 SUN	WORKING		9 WED		
10 THU	C/RD	B/E	10 SUN	WORKING		10 MON			10 THU		
11 FRI	C/E	B/RD	11 MON			11 TUE			11 FRI		
12 SAT	WORKING		12 TUE			12 WED			12 SAT	OFF	
13 SUN	WORKING		13 WED			13 THU			13 SUN	OFF	
14 MON			14 THU			14 FRI			14 MON		
15 TUE			15 FRI			15 SAT	OFF		15 TUE		
16 WED			16 SAT	OFF		16 SUN	OFF		16 WED		
17 THU			17 SUN	OFF		17 MON			17 THU		
18 FRI			18 MON			18 TUE			18 FRI		
19 SAT	OFF		19 TUE			19 WED			19 SAT	WORKING	
20 SUN	OFF		20 WED			20 THU			20 SUN	WORKING	
21 MON			21 THU			21 FRI			21 MON		
22 TUE			22 FRI			22 SAT	WORKING		22 TUE		
23 WED			23 SAT	WORKING		23 SUN	WORKING		23 WED		
24 THU			24 SUN	WORKING		24 MON			24 THU		
25 FRI			25 MON			25 TUE			25 FRI		
26 SAT	WORKING		26 TUE			26 WED			26 SAT	OFF	
27 SUN	WORKING		27 WED			27 THU			27 SUN	OFF	
28 MON			28 THU			28 FRI			28 MON		
29 TUE			29 FRI			29 SAT	OFF		29 TUE		
30 WED						30 SUN	OFF		30 WED		
31 THU						31 MON					

2008 YEAR PLANNER

MAY		JUNE		JULY		AUGUST	
1 THU		1 SUN	WORKING	1 TUE		1 FRI	
2 FRI		2 MON		2 WED		2 SAT	OFF
3 SAT	WORKING	3 TUE		3 THU		3 SUN	OFF
4 SUN	WORKING	4 WED		4 FRI		4 MON	
5 MON		5 THU		5 SAT	OFF	5 TUE	
6 TUE		6 FRI		6 SUN	OFF	6 WED	
7 WED		7 SAT	OFF	7 MON		7 THU	
8 THU		8 SUN	OFF	8 TUE		8 FRI	
9 FRI		9 MON		9 WED		9 SAT	WORKING
10 SAT	OFF	10 TUE		10 THU		10 SUN	WORKING
11 SUN	OFF	11 WED		11 FRI		11 MON	
12 MON		12 THU		12 SAT	WORKING	12 TUE	
13 TUE		13 FRI		13 SUN	WORKING	13 WED	
14 WED		14 SAT	WORKING	14 MON		14 THU	
15 THU		15 SUN	WORKING	15 TUE		15 FRI	
16 FRI		16 MON		16 WED		16 SAT	OFF
17 SAT	WORKING	17 TUE		17 THU		17 SUN	OFF
18 SUN	WORKING	18 WED		18 FRI		18 MON	
19 MON		19 THU		19 SAT	OFF	19 TUE	
20 TUE		20 FRI		20 SUN	OFF	20 WED	
21 WED		21 SAT	OFF	21 MON		21 THU	
22 THU		22 SUN	OFF	22 TUE		22 FRI	
23 FRI		23 MON		23 WED		23 SAT	WORKING
24 SAT	OFF	24 TUE		24 THU		24 SUN	WORKING
25 SUN	OFF	25 WED		25 FRI		25 MON	
26 MON		26 THU		26 SAT	WORKING	26 TUE	
27 TUE		27 FRI		27 SUN	WORKING	27 WED	
28 WED		28 SAT	WORKING	28 MON		28 THU	
29 THU		29 SUN	WORKING	29 TUE		29 FRI	
30 FRI		30 MON		30 WED		30 SAT	OFF
31 SAT	WORKING			31 THU		31 SUN	OFF

2008 YEAR PLANNER

SEPTEMBER		OCTOBER		NOVEMBER		DECEMBER	
1 MON		1 WED		1 SAT	WORKING	1 MON	
2 TUE		2 THU		2 SUN	WORKING	2 TUE	
3 WED		3 FRI		3 MON		3 WED	
4 THU		4 SAT	WORKING	4 TUE		4 THU	
5 FRI		5 SUN	WORKING	5 WED		5 FRI	
6 SAT	WORKING	6 MON		6 THU		6 SAT	OFF
7 SUN	WORKING	7 TUE		7 FRI		7 SUN	OFF
8 MON		8 WED		8 SAT	OFF	8 MON	
9 TUE		9 THU		9 SUN	OFF	9 TUE	
10 WED		10 FRI		10 MON		10 WED	
11 THU		11 SAT	OFF	11 TUE		11 THU	
12 FRI		12 SUN	OFF	12 WED		12 FRI	
13 SAT	OFF	13 MON		13 THU		13 SAT	WORKING
14 SUN	OFF	14 TUE		14 FRI		14 SUN	WORKING
15 MON		15 WED		15 SAT	WORKING	15 MON	
16 TUE		16 THU		16 SUN	WORKING	16 TUE	
17 WED		17 FRI		17 MON		17 WED	
18 THU		18 SAT	WORKING	18 TUE		18 THU	
19 FRI		19 SUN	WORKING	19 WED		19 FRI	
20 SAT	WORKING	20 MON		20 THU		20 SAT	OFF
21 SUN	WORKING	21 TUE		21 FRI		21 SUN	OFF
22 MON		22 WED		22 SAT	OFF	22 MON	
23 TUE		23 THU		23 SUN	OFF	23 TUE	
24 WED		24 FRI		24 MON		24 WED	
25 THU		25 SAT	OFF	25 TUE		25 THU	
26 FRI		26 SUN	OFF	26 WED		26 FRI	
27 SAT	OFF	27 MON		27 THU		27 SAT	WORKING
28 SUN	OFF	28 TUE		28 FRI		28 SUN	WORKING
29 MON		29 WED		29 SAT	WORKING	29 MON	
30 TUE		30 THU		30 SUN	WORKING	30 TUE	
		31 FRI				31 WED	

30
sun
dim.dom.son

Last Quarter ◑ 7:51 U.T.

31
mon
lun.lun.mon

New Year's Eve
Saint-Sylvestre
Fin de Año
Silvester

JANUARY . JANVIER . ENERO . JANUAR 2008

1
tue
mar.mar.die

New Year's Day
Jour de l'An
Año Nuevo
Neujahr
Kwanzaa ends

2
wed
mer.miér.mit

Day after New Year's Day (NZ; SCT)

3
thu
jeu.jue.don

4
fri
ven.vier.fre

7.30 PM. QUEENS ISLAND (NI PUP OF THE YEAR)
KNOCKMORE ROAD LISBURN DID NOT ATTEND

5
sat
sam.sáb.sam

©2007 Randi Hirschmann

DECEMBER 2007						
						1
2	3	4	5	6	7	8
9	10	11	12	13	14	15
16	17	18	19	20	21	22
23	24	25	26	27	28	29
30	31					

JANUARY 2008						
	1	2	3	4	5	
6	7	8	9	10	11	12
13	14	15	16	17	18	19
20	21	22	23	24	25	26
27	28	29	30	31		

FEBRUARY 2008						
					1	2
3	4	5	6	7	8	9
10	11	12	13	14	15	16
17	18	19	20	21	22	23
24	25	26	27	28	29	

DECEMBER 2007	JANUARY 2008	FEBRUARY 2008
1	1 2 3 4 5	1 2
2 3 4 5 6 7 8	6 7 8 9 10 11 12	3 4 5 6 7 8 9
9 10 11 12 13 14 15	13 14 15 16 17 18 19	10 11 12 13 14 15 16
16 17 18 19 20 21 22	20 21 22 23 24 25 26	17 18 19 20 21 22 23
23 24 25 26 27 28 29	27 28 29 30 31	24 25 26 27 28 29
30 31		

6
sun
dim.dom.son

Epiphany
Épiphanie
Día de los Reyes
Heilige Drei Könige

7
mon
lun.lun.mon

New Moon ◯ 11:37 U.T.

8
tue
mar.mar.die

9
wed
mer.miér.mit

10
thu
jeu.jue.don

11
fri
ven.vier.fre

12
sat
sam.sáb.sam

13
s u n
dim.dom.son

14
m o n
lun.lun.mon

Coming of Age Day (JP)
Natalicio de Eugenio María de Hostos (PR)

First Quarter ◐ 19:46 U.T.

15
t u e
mar.mar.die

16
w e d
mer.miér.mit

17
t h u
jeu.jue.don

18
f r i
ven.vier.fre

19
s a t
sam.sáb.sam

(N I) PASTORAL/WORKING PUPPY OF THE YEAR.
11:30 AM   BALMORAL HOTEL

©2007 Mark Raycroft

DECEMBER 2007	JANUARY 2008	FEBRUARY 2008
1	1 2 3 4 5	1 2
2 3 4 5 6 7 8	6 7 8 9 10 11 12	3 4 5 6 7 8 9
9 10 11 12 13 14 15	13 14 15 16 17 18 19	10 11 12 13 14 15 16
16 17 18 19 20 21 22	20 21 22 23 24 25 26	17 18 19 20 21 22 23
23 24 25 26 27 28 29	27 28 29 30 31	24 25 26 27 28 29
30 31		

©2007 Cheryl A. Ertelt

DECEMBER 2007	JANUARY 2008	FEBRUARY 2008
1	1 2 3 4 5	1 2
2 3 4 5 6 7 8	6 7 8 9 10 11 12	3 4 5 6 7 8 9
9 10 11 12 13 14 15	13 14 15 16 17 18 19	10 11 12 13 14 15 16
16 17 18 19 20 21 22	20 21 22 23 24 25 26	17 18 19 20 21 22 23
23 24 25 26 27 28 29	27 28 29 30 31	24 25 26 27 28 29
30 31		

20
sun
dim.dom.son

21
mon
lun.lun.mon

Martin Luther King, Jr. Day (US)

Full Moon ◖ 13:35 U.T.

22
tue
mar.mar.die

23
wed
mer.miér.mit

24
thu
jeu.jue.don

25
fri
ven.vier.fre

Burns Night (SCT)

26
sat
sam.sáb.sam

NON SPORTING BREEDS
COMBER LEISURE CENTRE
 10am

27
sun
dim.dom.son

Holocaust Memorial Day (UN)

28
mon
lun.lun.mon

Australia Day (AU)

29
tue
mar.mar.die

Last Quarter ◑ 5:03 U.T.

30
wed
mer.miér.mit

31
thu
jeu.jue.don

1
fri
ven.vier.fre

2
sat
sam.sáb.sam

Groundhog Day
Día de la Candelaria (MX)

week 5

JANUARY 2008

					1	2	3	4	5
6	7	8	9	10	11	12
13	14	15	16	17	18	19
20	21	22	23	24	25	26
27	28	29	30	31

FEBRUARY 2008

					1	2
3	4	5	6	7	8	9
10	11	12	13	14	15	16
17	18	19	20	21	22	23
24	25	26	27	28	29

MARCH 2008

						1
2	3	4	5	6	7	8
9	10	11	12	13	14	15
16	17	18	19	20	21	22
23	24	25	26	27	28	29
30	31

JANUARY 2008	FEBRUARY 2008	MARCH 2008
1 2 3 4 5	1 2	1
6 7 8 9 10 11 12	3 4 5 6 7 8 9	2 3 4 5 6 7 8
13 14 15 16 17 18 19	10 11 12 13 14 15 16	9 10 11 12 13 14 15
20 21 22 23 24 25 26	17 18 19 20 21 22 23	16 17 18 19 20 21 22
27 28 29 30 31	24 25 26 27 28 29	23 24 25 26 27 28 29
		30 31

3
sun
dim.dom.son

4
mon
lun.lun.mon

5
tue
mar.mar.die

Shrove Tuesday
Fat Tuesday
Mardi gras
Martes de Carnaval
Fastnacht
Día de la Constitución (MX)

6
wed
mer.miér.mit

Ash Wednesday
Mercredi des Cendres
Miércoles de Ceniza
Aschermittwoch
Waitangi Day (NZ)

7
thu
jeu.jue.don

New Moon ◯ 3:44 U.T.
Solar Eclipse (Annular) 3:55 U.T.

Chinese New Year - Year of the Rat

8
fri
ven.vier.fre

9
sat
sam.sáb.sam

10
sun
dim.dom.son

11
mon
lun.lun.mon

National Foundation Day (JP)

12
tue
mar.mar.die

Lincoln's Birthday (US)

13
wed
mer.miér.mit

First Quarter ◑ 3:33 U.T.

14
thu
jeu.jue.don

Valentine's Day
Saint-Valentin
Día del Amor y la Amistad (MX)
Valentinstag

15
fri
ven.vier.fre

16
sat
sam.sáb.sam

JANUARY 2008							FEBRUARY 2008							MARCH 2008						
		1	2	3	4	5						1	2							1
6	7	8	9	10	11	12	3	4	5	6	7	8	9	2	3	4	5	6	7	8
13	14	15	16	17	18	19	10	11	12	13	14	15	16	9	10	11	12	13	14	15
20	21	22	23	24	25	26	17	18	19	20	21	22	23	16	17	18	19	20	21	22
27	28	29	30	31			24	25	26	27	28	29		23	24	25	26	27	28	29
														30	31					

JANUARY 2008	FEBRUARY 2008	MARCH 2008
1 2 3 4 5	1 2	1
6 7 8 9 10 11 12	3 4 5 6 7 8 9	2 3 4 5 6 7 8
13 14 15 16 17 18 19	10 11 12 13 14 15 16	9 10 11 12 13 14 15
20 21 22 23 24 25 26	17 18 19 20 21 22 23	16 17 18 19 20 21 22
27 28 29 30 31	24 25 26 27 28 29	23 24 25 26 27 28 29
		30 31

17
sun
dim.dom.son

18
mon
lun.lun.mon

Presidents' Day (US)
Family Day (AB, CAN)
Natalicio de Luis Muñoz Marín (PR)

19
tue
mar.mar.die

20
wed
mer.miér.mit

Full Moon ● 3:30 U.T.
Lunar Eclipse (Total) 3:26 U.T.

21
thu
jeu.jue.don

Chinese Lantern Festival

22
fri
ven.vier.fre

Washington's Birthday (US)

23
sat
sam.sáb.sam

NEWTOWNARDS   CH SHOW   —   BALMORAL

24
sun
dim.dom.son

Día de la Bandera (MX)

25
mon
lun.lun.mon

26
tue
mar.mar.die

27
wed
mer.miér.mit

28
thu
jeu.jue.don

Last Quarter ◗ 2:18 U.T.

29
fri
ven.vier.fre

MARCH . MARS . MARZO . MÄRZ 2008

1
sat
sam.sáb.sam

St. David's Day (WAL)
Independence Movement (KR)

FEBRUARY 2008						
					1	2
3	4	5	6	7	8	9
10	11	12	13	14	15	16
17	18	19	20	21	22	23
24	25	26	27	28	29	

MARCH 2008						
						1
2	3	4	5	6	7	8
9	10	11	12	13	14	15
16	17	18	19	20	21	22
23	24	25	26	27	28	29
30	31					

APRIL 2008						
		1	2	3	4	5
6	7	8	9	10	11	12
13	14	15	16	17	18	19
20	21	22	23	24	25	26
27	28	29	30			

FEBRUARY 2008	MARCH 2008	APRIL 2008
1 2	1	1 2 3 4 5
3 4 5 6 7 8 9	2 3 4 5 6 7 8	6 7 8 9 10 11 12
10 11 12 13 14 15 16	9 10 11 12 13 14 15	13 14 15 16 17 18 19
17 18 19 20 21 22 23	16 17 18 19 20 21 22	20 21 22 23 24 25 26
24 25 26 27 28 29	23 24 25 26 27 28 29	27 28 29 30
	30 31	

2
sun
dim.dom.son

Mothering Sunday (UK)

3
mon
lun.lun.mon

Labour Day (WA, AU)

4
tue
mar.mar.die

5
wed
mer.miér.mit

6
thu
jeu.jue.don

New Moon ◯ 17:14 U.T.

7
fri
ven.vier.fre

8
sat
sam.sáb.sam

International Women's Day

9
sun
dim.dom.son

Daylight Saving Time begins (US; CAN)

10
mon
lun.lun.mon

Labour Day (VIC, AU)
Eight Hours Day (TAS, AU)
Great Lent begins (Orthodox)

11
tue
mar.mar.die

12
wed
mer.miér.mit

13
thu
jeu.jue.don

First Quarter 🌓 10:46 U.T.

14
fri
ven.vier.fre

15
sat
sam.sáb.sam

FEBRUARY 2008

					1	2
3	4	5	6	7	8	9
10	11	12	13	14	15	16
17	18	19	20	21	22	23
24	25	26	27	28	29	

MARCH 2008

						1
2	3	4	5	6	7	8
9	10	11	12	13	14	15
16	17	18	19	20	21	22
23	24	25	26	27	28	29
30	31					

APRIL 2008

		1	2	3	4	5
6	7	8	9	10	11	12
13	14	15	16	17	18	19
20	21	22	23	24	25	26
27	28	29	30			

FEBRUARY 2008							MARCH 2008							APRIL 2008					
					1	2							1			1	2	3	4	5
3	4	5	6	7	8	9	2	3	4	5	6	7	8	6	7	8	9	10	11	12
10	11	12	13	14	15	16	9	10	11	12	13	14	15	13	14	15	16	17	18	19
17	18	19	20	21	22	23	16	17	18	19	20	21	22	20	21	22	23	24	25	26
24	25	26	27	28	29		23	24	25	26	27	28	29	27	28	29	30			
							30	31												

16
sun
dim.dom.son

Palm Sunday
Dimanche des Rameaux
Domingo de Ramos

17
mon
lun.lun.mon

St. Patrick's Day
Saint-Patrick
San Patricio

18
tue
mar.mar.die

19
wed
mer.miér.mit

20
thu
jeu.jue.don

Vernal Equinox
Équinoxe du printemps
Equinoccio de Primavera
5:48 U.T.

Maundy Thursday   Jeudi saint   Jueves Santo
Journée internationale de la Francophonie (Int'l Speakers of French Day)

Full Moon 18:40 U.T.

21
fri
ven.vier.fre

Good Friday   Vendredi saint   Viernes Santo   Karfreitag
Bank Holiday (UK)
Natalicio de Benito Juárez (MX)

22
sat
sam.sáb.sam

Holy Saturday
Samedi saint
Sábado de Gloria
Día de la Abolición de la Esclavitud (PR)

23
sun
dim.dom.son

Easter Sunday
Pâques
Domingo de Pascua
Ostersonntag

24
mon
lun.lun.mon

Easter Monday
Lundi de Pâques
Lunes de Pascua
Ostermontag
Bank Holiday (UK except SCT)

25
tue
mar.mar.die

26
wed
mer.miér.mit

27
thu
jeu.jue.don

28
fri
ven.vier.fre

Last Quarter ◗ 21:47 U.T.

29
sat
sam.sáb.sam

FEBRUARY 2008	MARCH 2008	APRIL 2008
1 2	1	1 2 3 4 5
3 4 5 6 7 8 9	2 3 4 5 6 7 8	6 7 8 9 10 11 12
10 11 12 13 14 15 16	9 10 11 12 13 14 15	13 14 15 16 17 18 19
17 18 19 20 21 22 23	16 17 18 19 20 21 22	20 21 22 23 24 25 26
24 25 26 27 28 29	23 24 25 26 27 28 29	27 28 29 30
	30 31	

MARCH 2008	APRIL 2008	MAY 2008
1	1 2 3 4 5	1 2 3
2 3 4 5 6 7 8	6 7 8 9 10 11 12	4 5 6 7 8 9 10
9 10 11 12 13 14 15	13 14 15 16 17 18 19	11 12 13 14 15 16 17
16 17 18 19 20 21 22	20 21 22 23 24 25 26	18 19 20 21 22 23 24
23 24 25 26 27 28 29	27 28 29 30	25 26 27 28 29 30 31
30 31		

30
sun
dim.dom.son

European Union Daylight Saving Time begins

31
mon
lun.lun.mon

APRIL . AVRIL . ABRIL . APRIL   2008

1
tue
mar.mar.die

April Fools' Day

2
wed
mer.miér.mit

3
thu
jeu.jue.don

4
fri
ven.vier.fre

5
sat
sam.sáb.sam

Day of Trees (KR)

New Moon ◯ 3:55 U.T.

6
s u n
dim.dom.son

7
m o n
lun.lun.mon

8
t u e
mar.mar.die

9
w e d
mer.miér.mit

10
t h u
jeu.jue.don

11
f r i
ven.vier.fre

First Quarter ◑ 18:32 U.T.

12
s a t
sam.sáb.sam

MARCH 2008						
						1
2	3	4	5	6	7	8
9	10	11	12	13	14	15
16	17	18	19	20	21	22
23	24	25	26	27	28	29
30	31					

APRIL 2008						
		1	2	3	4	5
6	7	8	9	10	11	12
13	14	15	16	17	18	19
20	21	22	23	24	25	26
27	28	29	30			

MAY 2008						
				1	2	3
4	5	6	7	8	9	10
11	12	13	14	15	16	17
18	19	20	21	22	23	24
25	26	27	28	29	30	31

MARCH 2008

						1
2	3	4	5	6	7	8
9	10	11	12	13	14	15
16	17	18	19	20	21	22
23	24	25	26	27	28	29
30	31					

APRIL 2008

		1	2	3	4	5
6	7	8	9	10	11	12
13	14	15	16	17	18	19
20	21	22	23	24	25	26
27	28	29	30			

MAY 2008

				1	2	3
4	5	6	7	8	9	10
11	12	13	14	15	16	17
18	19	20	21	22	23	24
25	26	27	28	29	30	31

13
sun
dim.dom.son

14
mon
lun.lun.mon

15
tue
mar.mar.die

16
wed
mer.miér.mit

17
thu
jeu.jue.don

18
fri
ven.vier.fre

19
sat
sam.sáb.sam

Passover begins at sundown

Full Moon ● 10:25 U.T.

20
sun
dim.dom.son

21
mon
lun.lun.mon

Día de la Reafirmación del Idioma Español (PR)
Natalicio de José de Diego (PR)

22
tue
mar.mar.die

Earth Day

23
wed
mer.miér.mit

St. George's Day (ENG)

24
thu
jeu.jue.don

25
fri
ven.vier.fre

ANZAC Day (AU; NZ)
Arbor Day (US)

26
sat
sam.sáb.sam

MARCH 2008						
						1
2	3	4	5	6	7	8
9	10	11	12	13	14	15
16	17	18	19	20	21	22
23	24	25	26	27	28	29
30	31					

APRIL 2008						
	1	2	3	4	5	
6	7	8	9	10	11	12
13	14	15	16	17	18	19
20	21	22	23	24	25	26
27	28	29	30			

MAY 2008						
					1	2	3
4	5	6	7	8	9	10
11	12	13	14	15	16	17
18	19	20	21	22	23	24
25	26	27	28	29	30	31

APRIL 2008	MAY 2008	JUNE 2008
1 2 3 4 5	1 2 3	1 2 3 4 5 6 7
6 7 8 9 10 11 12	4 5 6 7 8 9 10	8 9 10 11 12 13 14
13 14 15 16 17 18 19	11 12 13 14 15 16 17	15 16 17 18 19 20 21
20 21 22 23 24 25 26	18 19 20 21 22 23 24	22 23 24 25 26 27 28
27 28 29 30	25 26 27 28 29 30 31	29 30

27
sun
dim.dom.son

Pascha (Orthodox)

Last Quarter ◗ 14:12 U.T.

28
mon
lun.lun.mon

29
tue
mar.mar.die

Green Day (JP)

30
wed
mer.miér.mit

Koninginnedag (NL)
Día del Niño (MX)

MAY . MAI . MAYO . MAI   2008

1
thu
jeu.jue.don

May Day   Maifeiertag (DE)
International Worker's Day
Fête du Travail (FR)
Día del Trabajo (MX)
Ascension Ascensión Himmelfahrt Hemelvaart (NL)

2
fri
ven.vier.fre

3
sat
sam.sáb.sam

Constitution Day (JP)

4
sun
dim.dom.son

Dodenherdenking (NL)

5
mon
lun.lun.mon

(P H)

New Moon ◯ 12:18 U.T.
Batalla de Puebla (MX)
Bevrijdingsdag (NL)
Children's Day (JP; KR)
Early May Bank Holiday (IRL; UK)
Labour Day (QLD, AU)   May Day (NT, AU)

6
tue
mar.mar.die

7
wed
mer.miér.mit

8
thu
jeu.jue.don

Fête de la Victoire (FR)

9
fri
ven.vier.fre

Europe Day (EU)

10
sat
sam.sáb.sam

Día de las Madres (MX)

APRIL 2008						
		1	2	3	4	5
6	7	8	9	10	11	12
13	14	15	16	17	18	19
20	21	22	23	24	25	26
27	28	29	30			

MAY 2008						
				1	2	3
4	5	6	7	8	9	10
11	12	13	14	15	16	17
18	19	20	21	22	23	24
25	26	27	28	29	30	31

JUNE 2008						
1	2	3	4	5	6	7
8	9	10	11	12	13	14
15	16	17	18	19	20	21
22	23	24	25	26	27	28
29	30					

APRIL 2008

		1	2	3	4	5
6	7	8	9	10	11	12
13	14	15	16	17	18	19
20	21	22	23	24	25	26
27	28	29	30			

MAY 2008

				1	2	3
4	5	6	7	8	9	10
11	12	13	14	15	16	17
18	19	20	21	22	23	24
25	26	27	28	29	30	31

JUNE 2008

1	2	3	4	5	6	7
8	9	10	11	12	13	14
15	16	17	18	19	20	21
22	23	24	25	26	27	28
29	30					

11
sun
dim.dom.son

Mother's Day (US; AU; CAN; NZ)
Fête des Mères (CAN)
Moederdag (NL)
Pentecost Pentecôte Pentecostés Pfingstsonntag Pinksteren (NL)

First Quarter ◑ 3:47 U.T.

12
mon
lun.lun.mon

Pentecost (Whit) Monday
Lundi de Pentecôte
Lunes de Pentecostés
Pfingstmontag

13
tue
mar.mar.die

14
wed
mer.miér.mit

15
thu
jeu.jue.don

Día del Maestro (MX)

16
fri
ven.vier.fre

17
sat
sam.sáb.sam

18
sun
dim.dom.son

19
mon
lun.lun.mon

Victoria Day (CAN)
La Journée nationale des patriotes (QC, CAN)

Full Moon 🌕 2:11 U.T.

20
tue
mar.mar.die

21
wed
mer.miér.mit

22
thu
jeu.jue.don

Fronleichnam (DE)

23
fri
ven.vier.fre

24
sat
sam.sáb.sam

APRIL 2008

		1	2	3	4	5
6	7	8	9	10	11	12
13	14	15	16	17	18	19
20	21	22	23	24	25	26
27	28	29	30			

MAY 2008

				1	2	3
4	5	6	7	8	9	10
11	12	13	14	15	16	17
18	19	20	21	22	23	24
25	26	27	28	29	30	31

JUNE 2008

1	2	3	4	5	6	7
8	9	10	11	12	13	14
15	16	17	18	19	20	21
22	23	24	25	26	27	28
29	30					

APRIL 2008
1 2 3 4 5
6 7 8 9 10 11 12
13 14 15 16 17 18 19
20 21 22 23 24 25 26
27 28 29 30

MAY 2008
1 2 3
4 5 6 7 8 9 10
11 12 13 14 15 16 17
18 19 20 21 22 23 24
25 26 27 28 29 30 31

JUNE 2008
1 2 3 4 5 6 7
8 9 10 11 12 13 14
15 16 17 18 19 20 21
22 23 24 25 26 27 28
29 30

25
sun
dim.dom.son

Fête des Mères (FR)

26
mon
lun.lun.mon

Memorial Day (US)
Día de la Recordación de los Muertos de la Guerra (PR)
Spring Bank Holiday (UK)

27
tue
mar.mar.die

Last Quarter 2:57 U.T.

28
wed
mer.miér.mit

29
thu
jeu.jue.don

30
fri
ven.vier.fre

31
sat
sam.sáb.sam

1
sun
dim.dom.son

2
mon
lun.lun.mon

Bank Holiday (IRL)
Queen's Birthday (NZ)
Foundation Day (WA, AU)

New Moon ◯ 19:23 U.T.

3
tue
mar.mar.die

4
wed
mer.miér.mit

5
thu
jeu.jue.don

6
fri
ven.vier.fre

Memorial Day (KR)

7
sat
sam.sáb.sam

---

week 23

MAY 2008						
				1	2	3
4	5	6	7	8	9	10
11	12	13	14	15	16	17
18	19	20	21	22	23	24
25	26	27	28	29	30	31

JUNE 2008						
1	2	3	4	5	6	7
8	9	10	11	12	13	14
15	16	17	18	19	20	21
22	23	24	25	26	27	28
29	30					

JULY 2008						
		1	2	3	4	5
6	7	8	9	10	11	12
13	14	15	16	17	18	19
20	21	22	23	24	25	26
27	28	29	30	31		

©2007 Lynn M. Stone

MAY 2008

				1	2	3
4	5	6	7	8	9	10
11	12	13	14	15	16	17
18	19	20	21	22	23	24
25	26	27	28	29	30	31

JUNE 2008

1	2	3	4	5	6	7
8	9	10	11	12	13	14
15	16	17	18	19	20	21
22	23	24	25	26	27	28
29	30					

JULY 2008

		1	2	3	4	5
6	7	8	9	10	11	12
13	14	15	16	17	18	19
20	21	22	23	24	25	26
27	28	29	30	31		

8
sun
dim.dom.son

Chinese Dragon Boat Festival

9
mon
lun.lun.mon

Queen's Birthday (AU except WA)

First Quarter ◑ 15:04 U.T.

10
tue
mar.mar.die

11
wed
mer.miér.mit

12
thu
jeu.jue.don

13
fri
ven.vier.fre

14
sat
sam.sáb.sam

Flag Day (US)
Queen's Official Birthday (tentative) (UK)

15
sun
dim.dom.son

Father's Day (US; CAN; UK)
Fête des Pères (CAN; FR)
Día del Padre (MX)
Vaderdag (NL)

16
mon
lun.lun.mon

17
tue
mar.mar.die

Full Moon ◐ 17:30 U.T.

18
wed
mer.miér.mit

19
thu
jeu.jue.don

Summer Solstice
Solstice d'été
Solsticio de Verano
23:59 U.T.

20
fri
ven.vier.fre

21
sat
sam.sáb.sam

First Nations Day
Journée internationale des populations autochtones (CAN)

MAY 2008	JUNE 2008	JULY 2008
1 2 3	1 2 3 4 5 6 7	1 2 3 4 5
4 5 6 7 8 9 10	8 9 10 11 12 13 14	6 7 8 9 10 11 12
11 12 13 14 15 16 17	15 16 17 18 19 20 21	13 14 15 16 17 18 19
18 19 20 21 22 23 24	22 23 24 25 26 27 28	20 21 22 23 24 25 26
25 26 27 28 29 30 31	29 30	27 28 29 30 31

MAY 2008

			1	2	3
4	5	6	7	8	9	10
11	12	13	14	15	16	17
18	19	20	21	22	23	24
25	26	27	28	29	30	31

JUNE 2008

1	2	3	4	5	6	7
8	9	10	11	12	13	14
15	16	17	18	19	20	21
22	23	24	25	26	27	28
29	30

JULY 2008

		1	2	3	4	5
6	7	8	9	10	11	12
13	14	15	16	17	18	19
20	21	22	23	24	25	26
27	28	29	30	31

22
sun
dim.dom.son

23
mon
lun.lun.mon

Discovery Day (NL, CAN)
Fête nationale du Luxembourg (LU)

24
tue
mar.mar.die

Fête nationale du Québec
Quebec National Day
Saint-Jean Baptiste (QC, CAN)
Día de San Juan Bautista (PR)

25
wed
mer.miér.mit

Last Quarter 12:10 U.T.

26
thu
jeu.jue.don

27
fri
ven.vier.fre

28
sat
sam.sáb.sam

29
sun
dim.dom.son

30
mon
lun.lun.mon

JULY . JUILLET . JULIO . JULI   2008

1
tue
mar.mar.die

Canada Day
Fête du Canada (CAN)

2
wed
mer.miér.mit

New Moon ◯ 2:19 U.T.

3
thu
jeu.jue.don

4
fri
ven.vier.fre

Independence Day (US)

5
sat
sam.sáb.sam

JUNE 2008	JULY 2008	AUGUST 2008
1 2 3 4 5 6 7	1 2 3 4 5	1 2
8 9 10 11 12 13 14	6 7 8 9 10 11 12	3 4 5 6 7 8 9
15 16 17 18 19 20 21	13 14 15 16 17 18 19	10 11 12 13 14 15 16
22 23 24 25 26 27 28	20 21 22 23 24 25 26	17 18 19 20 21 22 23
29 30	27 28 29 30 31	24 25 26 27 28 29 30
		31

JUNE 2008	JULY 2008	AUGUST 2008
1 2 3 4 5 6 7	1 2 3 4 5	1 2
8 9 10 11 12 13 14	6 7 8 9 10 11 12	3 4 5 6 7 8 9
15 16 17 18 19 20 21	13 14 15 16 17 18 19	10 11 12 13 14 15 16
22 23 24 25 26 27 28	20 21 22 23 24 25 26	17 18 19 20 21 22 23
29 30	27 28 29 30 31	24 25 26 27 28 29 30
		31

JULY . JUILLET . JULIO . JULI

6
sun
dim.dom.son

7
mon
lun.lun.mon

8
tue
mar.mar.die

9
wed
mer.miér.mit

First Quarter 4:35 U.T.

10
thu
jeu.jue.don

11
fri
ven.vier.fre

Feest van de Vlaamse Gemeenschap (BE)

12
sat
sam.sáb.sam

13
sun
dim.dom.son

14

mon
lun.lun.mon

Fête nationale de la France (FR)
Public Holiday (NIR)

15
tue
mar.mar.die

16
wed
mer.miér.mit

17
thu
jeu.jue.don

Constitution Day (KR)

Full Moon 7:59 U.T.

18
fri
ven.vier.fre

19
sat
sam.sáb.sam

©2007 Sharon Eide & Elizabeth Flynn

JUNE 2008

1	2	3	4	5	6	7
8	9	10	11	12	13	14
15	16	17	18	19	20	21
22	23	24	25	26	27	28
29	30					

JULY 2008

		1	2	3	4	5
6	7	8	9	10	11	12
13	14	15	16	17	18	19
20	21	22	23	24	25	26
27	28	29	30	31		

AUGUST 2008

					1	2
3	4	5	6	7	8	9
10	11	12	13	14	15	16
17	18	19	20	21	22	23
24	25	26	27	28	29	30
31						

JUNE 2008

1	2	3	4	5	6	7
8	9	10	11	12	13	14
15	16	17	18	19	20	21
22	23	24	25	26	27	28
29	30					

JULY 2008

		1	2	3	4	5
6	7	8	9	10	11	12
13	14	15	16	17	18	19
20	21	22	23	24	25	26
27	28	29	30	31		

AUGUST 2008

					1	2
3	4	5	6	7	8	9
10	11	12	13	14	15	16
17	18	19	20	21	22	23
24	25	26	27	28	29	30
31						

20
sun
dim.dom.son

21
mon
lun.lun.mon

Ocean Day (JP)
Nationale feestdag
Fête nationale de la Belgique (BE)
Natalicio de Luis Muñoz Rivera (PR)

22
tue
mar.mar.die

23
wed
mer.miér.mit

24
thu
jeu.jue.don

Last Quarter ◑ 18:42 U.T.

25
fri
ven.vier.fre

Conmemoración del Estado Libre Asociado (PR)

26
sat
sam.sáb.sam

27
sun
dim.dom.son

Natalicio de José Celso Barbosa (PR)

28
mon
lun.lun.mon

29
tue
mar.mar.die

30
wed
mer.miér.mit

31
thu
jeu.jue.don

AUGUST . AOÛT . AGOSTO . AUGUST   2008

New Moon ◯ 10:13 U.T.
Solar Eclipse (Total) 10:21 U.T.

1
fri
ven.vier.fre

2
sat
sam.sáb.sam

JULY 2008	AUGUST 2008	SEPTEMBER 2008
1 2 3 4 5	1 2	1 2 3 4 5 6
6 7 8 9 10 11 12	3 4 5 6 7 8 9	7 8 9 10 11 12 13
13 14 15 16 17 18 19	10 11 12 13 14 15 16	14 15 16 17 18 19 20
20 21 22 23 24 25 26	17 18 19 20 21 22 23	21 22 23 24 25 26 27
27 28 29 30 31	24 25 26 27 28 29 30	28 29 30
	31	

JULY 2008

		1	2	3	4	5
6	7	8	9	10	11	12
13	14	15	16	17	18	19
20	21	22	23	24	25	26
27	28	29	30	31		

AUGUST 2008

					1	2
3	4	5	6	7	8	9
10	11	12	13	14	15	16
17	18	19	20	21	22	23
24	25	26	27	28	29	30
31						

SEPTEMBER 2008

	1	2	3	4	5	6
7	8	9	10	11	12	13
14	15	16	17	18	19	20
21	22	23	24	25	26	27
28	29	30				

3
sun
dim.dom.son

4
mon
lun.lun.mon

Summer Bank Holiday (IRL; SCT)
Civic Holiday
Congé civique (CAN)
Picnic Day (NT, AU)

5
tue
mar.mar.die

6
wed
mer.miér.mit

7
thu
jeu.jue.don

First Quarter 20:20 U.T.

8
fri
ven.vier.fre

9
sat
sam.sáb.sam

10
sun
dim.dom.son

11
mon
lun.lun.mon

12
tue
mar.mar.die

13
wed
mer.miér.mit

14
thu
jeu.jue.don

15
fri
ven.vier.fre

Liberation Day (KR)
Assumption
Assomption
Asunción de María
Mariä Himmelfahrt

Full Moon 21:16 U.T.
Lunar Eclipse (Partial) 21:10 U.T.

16
sat
sam.sáb.sam

JULY 2008

		1	2	3	4	5
6	7	8	9	10	11	12
13	14	15	16	17	18	19
20	21	22	23	24	25	26
27	28	29	30	31		

AUGUST 2008

					1	2
3	4	5	6	7	8	9
10	11	12	13	14	15	16
17	18	19	20	21	22	23
24	25	26	27	28	29	30
31						

SEPTEMBER 2008

	1	2	3	4	5	6
7	8	9	10	11	12	13
14	15	16	17	18	19	20
21	22	23	24	25	26	27
28	29	30				

JULY 2008						
	1	2	3	4	5	
6	7	8	9	10	11	12
13	14	15	16	17	18	19
20	21	22	23	24	25	26
27	28	29	30	31		

AUGUST 2008						
					1	2
3	4	5	6	7	8	9
10	11	12	13	14	15	16
17	18	19	20	21	22	23
24	25	26	27	28	29	30
31						

SEPTEMBER 2008						
	1	2	3	4	5	6
7	8	9	10	11	12	13
14	15	16	17	18	19	20
21	22	23	24	25	26	27
28	29	30				

17
sun
dim.dom.son

18
mon
lun.lun.mon

Discovery Day (YT, CAN)

19
tue
mar.mar.die

20
wed
mer.miér.mit

21
thu
jeu.jue.don

22
fri
ven.vier.fre

Last Quarter ◗ 23:50 U.T.

23
sat
sam.sáb.sam

24
sun
dim.dom.son

25
mon
lun.lun.mon

Summer Bank Holiday (UK except SCT)

26
tue
mar.mar.die

27
wed
mer.miér.mit

28
thu
jeu.jue.don

29
fri
ven.vier.fre

New Moon ◯ 19:58 U.T.

30
sat
sam.sáb.sam

JULY 2008	AUGUST 2008	SEPTEMBER 2008
1 2 3 4 5	1 2	1 2 3 4 5 6
6 7 8 9 10 11 12	3 4 5 6 7 8 9	7 8 9 10 11 12 13
13 14 15 16 17 18 19	10 11 12 13 14 15 16	14 15 16 17 18 19 20
20 21 22 23 24 25 26	17 18 19 20 21 22 23	21 22 23 24 25 26 27
27 28 29 30 31	24 25 26 27 28 29 30	28 29 30
	31	

AUGUST 2008

					1	2
3	4	5	6	7	8	9
10	11	12	13	14	15	16
17	18	19	20	21	22	23
24	25	26	27	28	29	30
31						

SEPTEMBER 2008

1	2	3	4	5	6
7	8	9	10	11	12	13
14	15	16	17	18	19	20
21	22	23	24	25	26	27
28	29	30				

OCTOBER 2008

		1	2	3	4
5	6	7	8	9	10	11
12	13	14	15	16	17	18
19	20	21	22	23	24	25
26	27	28	29	30	31	

31
sun
dim.dom.son

SEPTEMBER . SEPTEMBRE . SEPTIEMBRE . SEPTEMBER   2008

1
mon
lun.lun.mon

Labor Day (US)
Labour Day
Fête du Travail (CAN)

2
tue
mar.mar.die

3
wed
mer.miér.mit

4
thu
jeu.jue.don

5
fri
ven.vier.fre

6
sat
sam.sáb.sam

First Quarter ◗ 14:04 U.T.

7
sun
dim.dom.son

Father's Day (AU; NZ)

8
mon
lun.lun.mon

9
tue
mar.mar.die

10
wed
mer.miér.mit

11
thu
jeu.jue.don

12
fri
ven.vier.fre

13
sat
sam.sáb.sam

AUGUST 2008	SEPTEMBER 2008	OCTOBER 2008
1 2	1 2 3 4 5 6	1 2 3 4
3 4 5 6 7 8 9	7 8 9 10 11 12 13	5 6 7 8 9 10 11
10 11 12 13 14 15 16	14 15 16 17 18 19 20	12 13 14 15 16 17 18
17 18 19 20 21 22 23	21 22 23 24 25 26 27	19 20 21 22 23 24 25
24 25 26 27 28 29 30	28 29 30	26 27 28 29 30 31
31		

©2007 PiperAnne Worcester

14
sun
dim.dom.son

Chinese Autumn Festival
Chuseok begins at sundown (KR)

Full Moon   9:13 U.T.

15
mon
lun.lun.mon

Noche del Grito (MX)
Respect for the Aged Day (JP)

16
tue
mar.mar.die

Día de la Independencia (MX)

17
wed
mer.miér.mit

18
thu
jeu.jue.don

19
fri
ven.vier.fre

20
sat
sam.sáb.sam

21
sun
dim.dom.son

22
mon
lun.lun.mon

Last Quarter ◖ 5:04 U.T.
Autumnal Equinox
Équinoxe d'automne
Equinoccio de Otoño
15:44 U.T.

23
tue
mar.mar.die

24
wed
mer.miér.mit

25
thu
jeu.jue.don

26
fri
ven.vier.fre

27
sat
sam.sáb.sam

Fête de la Communauté française (BE)

©2007 Larry & Marge Grant

AUGUST 2008						
					1	2
3	4	5	6	7	8	9
10	11	12	13	14	15	16
17	18	19	20	21	22	23
24	25	26	27	28	29	30
31						

SEPTEMBER 2008						
1	2	3	4	5	6	
7	8	9	10	11	12	13
14	15	16	17	18	19	20
21	22	23	24	25	26	27
28	29	30				

OCTOBER 2008						
			1	2	3	4
5	6	7	8	9	10	11
12	13	14	15	16	17	18
19	20	21	22	23	24	25
26	27	28	29	30	31	

SEPTEMBER 2008

	1	2	3	4	5	6
7	8	9	10	11	12	13
14	15	16	17	18	19	20
21	22	23	24	25	26	27
28	29	30				

OCTOBER 2008

			1	2	3	4
5	6	7	8	9	10	11
12	13	14	15	16	17	18
19	20	21	22	23	24	25
26	27	28	29	30	31	

NOVEMBER 2008

						1
2	3	4	5	6	7	8
9	10	11	12	13	14	15
16	17	18	19	20	21	22
23	24	25	26	27	28	29
30						

28
sun
dim.dom.son

29
mon
lun.lun.mon

New Moon ◯ 8:12 U.T.

Queen's Birthday (WA, AU)
Rosh Hashanah begins at sundown

30
tue
mar.mar.die

OCTOBER . OCTOBRE . OCTUBRE . OKTOBER   2008

1
wed
mer.miér.mit

Eid al-Fitr begins at sundown

2
thu
jeu.jue.don

3
fri
ven.vier.fre

National Foundation Day (KR)
Tag der deutschen Einheit (DE)

4
sat
sam.sáb.sam

5
sun
dim.dom.son

6
mon
lun.lun.mon

Labour Day (ACT, NSW, SA - AU)

First Quarter ◐ 9:04 U.T.

7
tue
mar.mar.die

8
wed
mer.miér.mit

Yom Kippur begins at sundown

9
thu
jeu.jue.don

10
fri
ven.vier.fre

11
sat
sam.sáb.sam

SEPTEMBER 2008	OCTOBER 2008	NOVEMBER 2008
1 2 3 4 5 6	1 2 3 4	1
7 8 9 10 11 12 13	5 6 7 8 9 10 11	2 3 4 5 6 7 8
14 15 16 17 18 19 20	12 13 14 15 16 17 18	9 10 11 12 13 14 15
21 22 23 24 25 26 27	19 20 21 22 23 24 25	16 17 18 19 20 21 22
28 29 30	26 27 28 29 30 31	23 24 25 26 27 28 29
		30

SEPTEMBER 2008

		1	2	3	4	5	6
7	8	9	10	11	12	13
14	15	16	17	18	19	20
21	22	23	24	25	26	27
28	29	30

OCTOBER 2008

			1	2	3	4
5	6	7	8	9	10	11
12	13	14	15	16	17	18
19	20	21	22	23	24	25
26	27	28	29	30	31

NOVEMBER 2008

						1
2	3	4	5	6	7	8
9	10	11	12	13	14	15
16	17	18	19	20	21	22
23	24	25	26	27	28	29

12
sun
dim.dom.son

Día de la Raza (MX)

13
mon
lun.lun.mon

Thanksgiving Day
Action de grâce (CAN)
Columbus Day (US)
Health & Sports Day (JP)

Full Moon ◑ 20:02 U.T.

14
tue
mar.mar.die

15
wed
mer.miér.mit

16
thu
jeu.jue.don

17
fri
ven.vier.fre

18
sat
sam.sáb.sam

19
sun
dim.dom.son

20
mon
lun.lun.mon

Last Quarter 11:55 U.T.

21
tue
mar.mar.die

22
wed
mer.miér.mit

23
thu
jeu.jue.don

24
fri
ven.vier.fre

United Nations Day

25
sat
sam.sáb.sam

SEPTEMBER 2008	OCTOBER 2008	NOVEMBER 2008
1 2 3 4 5 6	1 2 3 4	1
7 8 9 10 11 12 13	5 6 7 8 9 10 11	2 3 4 5 6 7 8
14 15 16 17 18 19 20	12 13 14 15 16 17 18	9 10 11 12 13 14 15
21 22 23 24 25 26 27	19 20 21 22 23 24 25	16 17 18 19 20 21 22
28 29 30	26 27 28 29 30 31	23 24 25 26 27 28 29
		30

OCTOBER 2008	NOVEMBER 2008	DECEMBER 2008
1 2 3 4	1	1 2 3 4 5 6
5 6 7 8 9 10 11	2 3 4 5 6 7 8	7 8 9 10 11 12 13
12 13 14 15 16 17 18	9 10 11 12 13 14 15	14 15 16 17 18 19 20
19 20 21 22 23 24 25	16 17 18 19 20 21 22	21 22 23 24 25 26 27
26 27 28 29 30 31	23 24 25 26 27 28 29	28 29 30 31
	30	

26
sun
dim.dom.son

European Union Daylight Saving Time ends

27
mon
lun.lun.mon

Labour Day (NZ)

New Moon ◯ 23:14 U.T.

28
tue
mar.mar.die

29
wed
mer.miér.mit

30
thu
jeu.jue.don

31
fri
ven.vier.fre

Halloween
Reformationstag (DE)

NOVEMBER . NOVEMBRE . NOVIEMBRE . NOVEMBER   2008

1
sat
sam.sáb.sam

All Saints Day
Toussaint
Día de Todos los Santos
Allerheiligen

2
sun
dim.dom.son

All Souls Day
Día de los Muertos (MX)
Daylight Saving Time ends (US; CAN)

3
mon
lun.lun.mon

Culture Day (JP)

4
tue
mar.mar.die

Election Day (US)
Melbourne Cup Day (Melb, AU)

5
wed
mer.miér.mit

Bonfire Night (UK)

First Quarter ◗ 4:03 U.T.

6
thu
jeu.jue.don

7
fri
ven.vier.fre

8
sat
sam.sáb.sam

OCTOBER 2008	NOVEMBER 2008	DECEMBER 2008
1 2 3 4	1	1 2 3 4 5 6
5 6 7 8 9 10 11	2 3 4 5 6 7 8	7 8 9 10 11 12 13
12 13 14 15 16 17 18	9 10 11 12 13 14 15	14 15 16 17 18 19 20
19 20 21 22 23 24 25	16 17 18 19 20 21 22	21 22 23 24 25 26 27
26 27 28 29 30 31	23 24 25 26 27 28 29	28 29 30 31
	30	

OCTOBER 2008

				1	2	3	4
5	6	7	8	9	10	11
12	13	14	15	16	17	18
19	20	21	22	23	24	25
26	27	28	29	30	31

NOVEMBER 2008

						1
2	3	4	5	6	7	8
9	10	11	12	13	14	15
16	17	18	19	20	21	22
23	24	25	26	27	28	29
30

DECEMBER 2008

		1	2	3	4	5	6
7	8	9	10	11	12	13
14	15	16	17	18	19	20
21	22	23	24	25	26	27
28	29	30	31

9
sun
dim.dom.son

Remembrance Sunday (UK)

10
mon
lun.lun.mon

11
tue
mar.mar.die

Veterans' Day (US)
Remembrance Day (AU; CAN)
Jour du Souvenir (CAN)
Armistice (FR)
Wapenstilstandsdag (BE)

12
wed
mer.miér.mit

Full Moon ◑ 6:17 U.T.

13
thu
jeu.jue.don

14
fri
ven.vier.fre

15
sat
sam.sáb.sam

Dag van de Dynasty
Journée de la Dinasty (BE)

16
sun
dim.dom.son

17
mon
lun.lun.mon

18
tue
mar.mar.die

Last Quarter 🌗 21:31 U.T.

19
wed
mer.miér.mit

Buß- und Bettag (DE)
Día del Descubrimiento de Puerto Rico (PR)

20
thu
jeu.jue.don

Día de la Revolución Mexicana (MX)

21
fri
ven.vier.fre

22
sat
sam.sáb.sam

©2007 Tara Darling

OCTOBER 2008	NOVEMBER 2008	DECEMBER 2008
1 2 3 4	1	1 2 3 4 5 6
5 6 7 8 9 10 11	2 3 4 5 6 7 8	7 8 9 10 11 12 13
12 13 14 15 16 17 18	9 10 11 12 13 14 15	14 15 16 17 18 19 20
19 20 21 22 23 24 25	16 17 18 19 20 21 22	21 22 23 24 25 26 27
26 27 28 29 30 31	23 24 25 26 27 28 29	28 29 30 31
	30	

OCTOBER 2008	NOVEMBER 2008	DECEMBER 2008
1 2 3 4	1	1 2 3 4 5 6
5 6 7 8 9 10 11	2 3 4 5 6 7 8	7 8 9 10 11 12 13
12 13 14 15 16 17 18	9 10 11 12 13 14 15	14 15 16 17 18 19 20
19 20 21 22 23 24 25	16 17 18 19 20 21 22	21 22 23 24 25 26 27
26 27 28 29 30 31	23 24 25 26 27 28 29	28 29 30 31
	30	

23
sun
dim.dom.son

Labor Gratitude Day (JP)

24
mon
lun.lun.mon

25
tue
mar.mar.die

26
wed
mer.miér.mit

New Moon ◯ 16:55 U.T.

27
thu
jeu.jue.don

Thanksgiving Day (US)

28
fri
ven.vier.fre

29
sat
sam.sáb.sam

NOVEMBER . NOVEMBRE . NOVIEMBRE . NOVEMBER   2008

30
sun
dim.dom.son

St. Andrew's Day (SCT)
Advent
Avent
Adviento

DECEMBER . DÉCEMBRE . DICIEMBRE . DEZEMBER   2008

1
mon
lun.lun.mon

2
tue
mar.mar.die

3
wed
mer.miér.mit

4
thu
jeu.jue.don

First Quarter ◗ 21:26 U.T.

5
fri
ven.vier.fre

Sinterklaas (NL)

6
sat
sam.sáb.sam

Sinterklaas
Saint Nicolas (BE)

week 49

NOVEMBER 2008

						1
2	3	4	5	6	7	8
9	10	11	12	13	14	15
16	17	18	19	20	21	22
23	24	25	26	27	28	29
30						

DECEMBER 2008

	1	2	3	4	5	6
7	8	9	10	11	12	13
14	15	16	17	18	19	20
21	22	23	24	25	26	27
28	29	30	31			

JANUARY 2009

					1	2	3
4	5	6	7	8	9	10
11	12	13	14	15	16	17
18	19	20	21	22	23	24
25	26	27	28	29	30	31

NOVEMBER 2008	DECEMBER 2008	JANUARY 2009
1	1 2 3 4 5 6	1 2 3
2 3 4 5 6 7 8	7 8 9 10 11 12 13	4 5 6 7 8 9 10
9 10 11 12 13 14 15	14 15 16 17 18 19 20	11 12 13 14 15 16 17
16 17 18 19 20 21 22	21 22 23 24 25 26 27	18 19 20 21 22 23 24
23 24 25 26 27 28 29	28 29 30 31	25 26 27 28 29 30 31
30		

7
sun
dim.dom.son

8
mon
lun.lun.mon

Eid al-Adha begins at sundown

9
tue
mar.mar.die

10
wed
mer.miér.mit

11
thu
jeu.jue.don

Full Moon ◐ 16:37 U.T.

12
fri
ven.vier.fre

Día de la Virgen de Guadalupe (MX)

13
sat
sam.sáb.sam

14
sun
dim.dom.son

15
mon
lun.lun.mon

16
tue
mar.mar.die

Las Posadas (MX)

17
wed
mer.miér.mit

18
thu
jeu.jue.don

Last Quarter ◑ 10:29 U.T.

19
fri
ven.vier.fre

20
sat
sam.sáb.sam

©2007 Tara Darling

NOVEMBER 2008	DECEMBER 2008	JANUARY 2009
1	1 2 3 4 5 6	1 2 3
2 3 4 5 6 7 8	7 8 9 10 11 12 13	4 5 6 7 8 9 10
9 10 11 12 13 14 15	14 15 16 17 18 19 20	11 12 13 14 15 16 17
16 17 18 19 20 21 22	21 22 23 24 25 26 27	18 19 20 21 22 23 24
23 24 25 26 27 28 29	28 29 30 31	25 26 27 28 29 30 31
30		

NOVEMBER 2008	DECEMBER 2008	JANUARY 2009
1	1 2 3 4 5 6	1 2 3
2 3 4 5 6 7 8	7 8 9 10 11 12 13	4 5 6 7 8 9 10
9 10 11 12 13 14 15	14 15 16 17 18 19 20	11 12 13 14 15 16 17
16 17 18 19 20 21 22	21 22 23 24 25 26 27	18 19 20 21 22 23 24
23 24 25 26 27 28 29	28 29 30 31	25 26 27 28 29 30 31
30		

21
sun
dim.dom.son

Winter Solstice
Solstice d'hiver
Solsticio de Invierno
12:04 U.T.

Hanukkah begins at sundown

22
mon
lun.lun.mon

23
tue
mar.mar.die

Emperor's Birthday (JP)

24
wed
mer.miér.mit

Christmas Eve
Veille de Noël
Noche Buena
Heiligabend

25
thu
jeu.jue.don

Christmas Day
Noël
Navidad
Erster Weihnachtstag (DE)

26
fri
ven.vier.fre

Boxing Day
Lendemain de Noël
Kwanzaa begins
St. Stephen's Day (IRL; LU)
Zweiter Weihnachtstag (DE)

New Moon ◯ 12:22 U.T.

27
sat
sam.sáb.sam

28
sun
dim.dom.son

29
mon
lun.lun.mon

30
tue
mar.mar.die

31
wed
mer.miér.mit

New Year's Eve
Saint-Sylvestre
Fin de Año
Silvester

JANUARY . JANVIER . ENERO . JANUAR 2009

1
thu
jeu.jue.don

New Year's Day
Jour de l'An
Año Nuevo
Neujahr
Kwanzaa ends

2
fri
ven.vier.fre

Day after New Year's Day (NZ; SCT)

3
sat
sam.sáb.sam

DECEMBER 2008

	1	2	3	4	5	6
7	8	9	10	11	12	13
14	15	16	17	18	19	20
21	22	23	24	25	26	27
28	29	30	31			

JANUARY 2009

				1	2	3
4	5	6	7	8	9	10
11	12	13	14	15	16	17
18	19	20	21	22	23	24
25	26	27	28	29	30	31

FEBRUARY 2009

1	2	3	4	5	6	7
8	9	10	11	12	13	14
15	16	17	18	19	20	21
22	23	24	25	26	27	28

2009 YEAR PLANNER

JANUARY		FEBRUARY		MARCH		APRIL	
1	THU	1	SUN	1	SUN	1	WED
2	FRI	2	MON	2	MON	2	THU
3	SAT	3	TUE	3	TUE	3	FRI
4	SUN	4	WED	4	WED	4	SAT
5	MON	5	THU	5	THU	5	SUN
6	TUE	6	FRI	6	FRI	6	MON
7	WED	7	SAT	7	SAT	7	TUE
8	THU	8	SUN	8	SUN	8	WED
9	FRI	9	MON	9	MON	9	THU
10	SAT	10	TUE	10	TUE	10	FRI
11	SUN	11	WED	11	WED	11	SAT
12	MON	12	THU	12	THU	12	SUN
13	TUE	13	FRI	13	FRI	13	MON
14	WED	14	SAT	14	SAT	14	TUE
15	THU	15	SUN	15	SUN	15	WED
16	FRI	16	MON	16	MON	16	THU
17	SAT	17	TUE	17	TUE	17	FRI
18	SUN	18	WED	18	WED	18	SAT
19	MON	19	THU	19	THU	19	SUN
20	TUE	20	FRI	20	FRI	20	MON
21	WED	21	SAT	21	SAT	21	TUE
22	THU	22	SUN	22	SUN	22	WED
23	FRI	23	MON	23	MON	23	THU
24	SAT	24	TUE	24	TUE	24	FRI
25	SUN	25	WED	25	WED	25	SAT
26	MON	26	THU	26	THU	26	SUN
27	TUE	27	FRI	27	FRI	27	MON
28	WED	28	SAT	28	SAT	28	TUE
29	THU			29	SUN	29	WED
30	FRI			30	MON	30	THU
31	SAT			31	TUE		

2009 YEAR PLANNER

MAY		JUNE		JULY		AUGUST	
1	FRI	1	MON	1	WED	1	SAT
2	SAT	2	TUE	2	THU	2	SUN
3	SUN	3	WED	3	FRI	3	MON
4	MON	4	THU	4	SAT	4	TUE
5	TUE	5	FRI	5	SUN	5	WED
6	WED	6	SAT	6	MON	6	THU
7	THU	7	SUN	7	TUE	7	FRI
8	FRI	8	MON	8	WED	8	SAT
9	SAT	9	TUE	9	THU	9	SUN
10	SUN	10	WED	10	FRI	10	MON
11	MON	11	THU	11	SAT	11	TUE
12	TUE	12	FRI	12	SUN	12	WED
13	WED	13	SAT	13	MON	13	THU
14	THU	14	SUN	14	TUE	14	FRI
15	FRI	15	MON	15	WED	15	SAT
16	SAT	16	TUE	16	THU	16	SUN
17	SUN	17	WED	17	FRI	17	MON
18	MON	18	THU	18	SAT	18	TUE
19	TUE	19	FRI	19	SUN	19	WED
20	WED	20	SAT	20	MON	20	THU
21	THU	21	SUN	21	TUE	21	FRI
22	FRI	22	MON	22	WED	22	SAT
23	SAT	23	TUE	23	THU	23	SUN
24	SUN	24	WED	24	FRI	24	MON
25	MON	25	THU	25	SAT	25	TUE
26	TUE	26	FRI	26	SUN	26	WED
27	WED	27	SAT	27	MON	27	THU
28	THU	28	SUN	28	TUE	28	FRI
29	FRI	29	MON	29	WED	29	SAT
30	SAT	30	TUE	30	THU	30	SUN
31	SUN			31	FRI	31	MON

2009 YEAR PLANNER

SEPTEMBER	OCTOBER	NOVEMBER	DECEMBER
1 TUE	1 THU	1 SUN	1 TUE
2 WED	2 FRI	2 MON	2 WED
3 THU	3 SAT	3 TUE	3 THU
4 FRI	4 SUN	4 WED	4 FRI
5 SAT	5 MON	5 THU	5 SAT
6 SUN	6 TUE	6 FRI	6 SUN
7 MON	7 WED	7 SAT	7 MON
8 TUE	8 THU	8 SUN	8 TUE
9 WED	9 FRI	9 MON	9 WED
10 THU	10 SAT	10 TUE	10 THU
11 FRI	11 SUN	11 WED	11 FRI
12 SAT	12 MON	12 THU	12 SAT
13 SUN	13 TUE	13 FRI	13 SUN
14 MON	14 WED	14 SAT	14 MON
15 TUE	15 THU	15 SUN	15 TUE
16 WED	16 FRI	16 MON	16 WED
17 THU	17 SAT	17 TUE	17 THU
18 FRI	18 SUN	18 WED	18 FRI
19 SAT	19 MON	19 THU	19 SAT
20 SUN	20 TUE	20 FRI	20 SUN
21 MON	21 WED	21 SAT	21 MON
22 TUE	22 THU	22 SUN	22 TUE
23 WED	23 FRI	23 MON	23 WED
24 THU	24 SAT	24 TUE	24 THU
25 FRI	25 SUN	25 WED	25 FRI
26 SAT	26 MON	26 THU	26 SAT
27 SUN	27 TUE	27 FRI	27 SUN
28 MON	28 WED	28 SAT	28 MON
29 TUE	29 THU	29 SUN	29 TUE
30 WED	30 FRI	30 MON	30 WED
	31 SAT		31 THU

NOTES

NOTES

NOTES

NOTES

NOTES

NOTES

NOTES

NOTES

NOTES

NOTES

NOTES

NOTES

NOTES

NOTES